The Adventures of Scuba Jack
Copyright 2021 by Beth Costanzo
All rights reserved

When visiting your *local aquarium* or swimming while you are on vacation, I'm sure that you have seen a wide range of fascinating *sea creatures*. There is so much amazing life in our seas and oceans. Along with their looks, many of these *sea creatures* have interesting stories to tell. In fact, many of them have been on our planet longer than humans have. It's remarkable.

www.adventuresofscubajack.com

One of the coolest, most adorable, and most fascinating sea creatures in our world today is the *sea turtle*. The sea turtle, which is also sometimes called the marine turtle, is an animal that is worth examining further. So join us in looking at why the **sea turtle** is so special. With this knowledge in hand, you can show off how smart you are about one of our ocean's coolest creatures.

www.adventuresofscubajack.com

Some Fascinating Facts About Sea Turtles

www.adventuresofscubajack.com

When you first look at a **sea turtle**, one of the most striking things is its *appearance*. If you're like me, you think that the **sea turtle** is extremely cute. The largest **sea turtle** (called the *leatherback sea turtle*) is about six to nine feet long and three to five feet wide. Other **sea turtles** are smaller (they are about two to four feet long). As far as their weight, sea turtles can grow up to be super heavy. They can weigh up to 2000 pounds, so don't try lifting them if you see them in the wild!

www.adventuresofscubajack.com

In case you didn't catch it, there are *different species* of **sea turtles** out there. Specifically, there are *seven* different species. There is the **leatherback sea turtle** (like I just mentioned). But along with that, there is the **green sea turtle, loggerhead sea turtle, Kemp's ridley sea turtle, olive ridley sea turtle, hawksbill sea turtle,** and **flatback sea turtle**. While these seven species differ in their unique ways, males and females are the same size. Looking at a sea turtle in an aquarium or in the ocean, you won't be able to tell whether it is a male or female solely on its size.

Sea turtles have been on our planet for a very long time. The first sea turtles appeared nearly *150 million years ago*. These sea turtles were found near Europe, although others were found near Africa around that time. Along with being on our Earth for hundreds of millions of years, sea turtles live very long lives. They are almost like humans in that they live to about 70 years (or even more). Because of this, the **sea turtle** that you see in the wild or at your local aquarium is probably older than you. In fact, it may be older than your parents!

www.adventuresofscubajack.com

From here, let's talk about how **sea turtles** behave in the wild. One of the most interesting things is that **sea turtles** can *hold* their breath for a *very long time*. **Sea turtles** need air to breathe, so they have to go to the surface of the water. But that said, **sea turtles** spend most of their time underwater. A *sleeping* **sea turtle** can remain underwater for about four to seven hours. When **sea turtles** go to the surface to breathe, they can get all of the air they need in one breath. It is truly remarkable.

www.adventuresofscubajack.com

Sea turtles love to *travel*. They travel more than 10,000 miles every year. Part of this distance is for **sea turtles** moving to a particular area where they can have children. When the baby is ready to arrive, the female sea turtle goes to land to lay her eggs. Females lay up to 150 eggs every two to three years. That is a lot of children!

Now let's talk about something that is important to any animal: what they *eat*. **Sea turtles** eat things like jellyfish, crabs, shrimp, sponges, snails, algae, and mollusks. But along with eating these different fish, sea turtles also eat plants. This means that they are omnivores. Some of the plants that sea turtles eat include seagrasses and seaweed.

The good news for *adult* **sea turtles** is that they have *few predators*, meaning that there are few animals that are trying to eat them. Their biggest threats are sharks and crocodiles. *Younger* **sea turtles** are more vulnerable, however. Predators on land (like jaguars) sometimes attack female sea turtles who are laying their eggs.

www.adventuresofscubajack.com

Like I have mentioned, you will probably be able to see some **sea turtles** in your local aquarium. But if you want to try seeing some sea turtles in the wild, you may be in luck. If you live in the United States, you may see some **Kemp's ridley sea turtles** on the East Coast of the United States or near the Gulf of Mexico. If you are looking for the **flatback sea turtle**, however, you may need to go all the way to Australia.

Finally, one of the troubling things about **sea turtles** is that they are dying out. Three species of sea turtles have been called *"endangered"* or *"critically endangered"*. This basically means that these species are at risk of disappearing forever. There are many adults who are working hard to *save* these **sea turtles**. However, all of us need to work together to make sure that **sea turtles** don't die out and disappear from our planet.

More Quick Facts About the Sea Turtle

If you want to impress some of your friends or family members with more sea turtles facts, you're in luck. Here are eight more that you can use:

www.adventuresofscubajack.com

We can find sea turtles in all of our oceans except for the really cold polar regions.

The large body size of sea turtles protects them from predators (like sharks) in the ocean.

Whether a baby sea turtle is male or female depends on the sand temperature surrounding the eggs as they grow.

While it is illegal to hunt sea turtles, unfortunately, they are hunted around the world.

www.adventuresofscubajack.com

Sea turtles (especially green sea turtles) are one of the few creatures that eat seagrass.

Plastic is a continuing danger to sea turtles.

www.adventuresofscubajack.com

Injured sea turtles are often rescued, healed, and released back into the wild.

Some towns in Florida have specific sea turtle nesting sites to protect baby sea turtles.

---

www.adventuresofscubajack.com

SEA TURTLE FACTS

They've been around for a very, very long time.
The oldest known sea turtle fossils date back about 150 million years, making them some of the oldest creatures on Earth. Just for some context, dinosaurs became extinct 65 million years ago

There are seven species of sea turtles, six of which are either threatened or endangered.
Humans pose the biggest threat to a sea turtle's survival, which contributes to problems such as entanglement, habitat loss and consumption of their eggs.

They really love to travel.
Leatherback sea turtles can travel more than 10,000 miles every year.

They can grow to be suuuuuper heavy.
Leatherback sea turtles can weigh up to 2,000 pounds.

Females lay up to 150 eggs every two to three years.
A couple months later, tiny turtles emerge.

For sea turtles, home is where the heart is.
When it's time to lay their eggs, female sea turtles return to the same nesting grounds where they were born.

They can hold their breath for a very (very, very) long time.
Green sea turtles can stay underwater for up to five hours, but their feeding dives usually only last five minutes or less.

Trace the word below:

SEA TURTLE

www.adventuresofscubajack.com

Trace the numbers

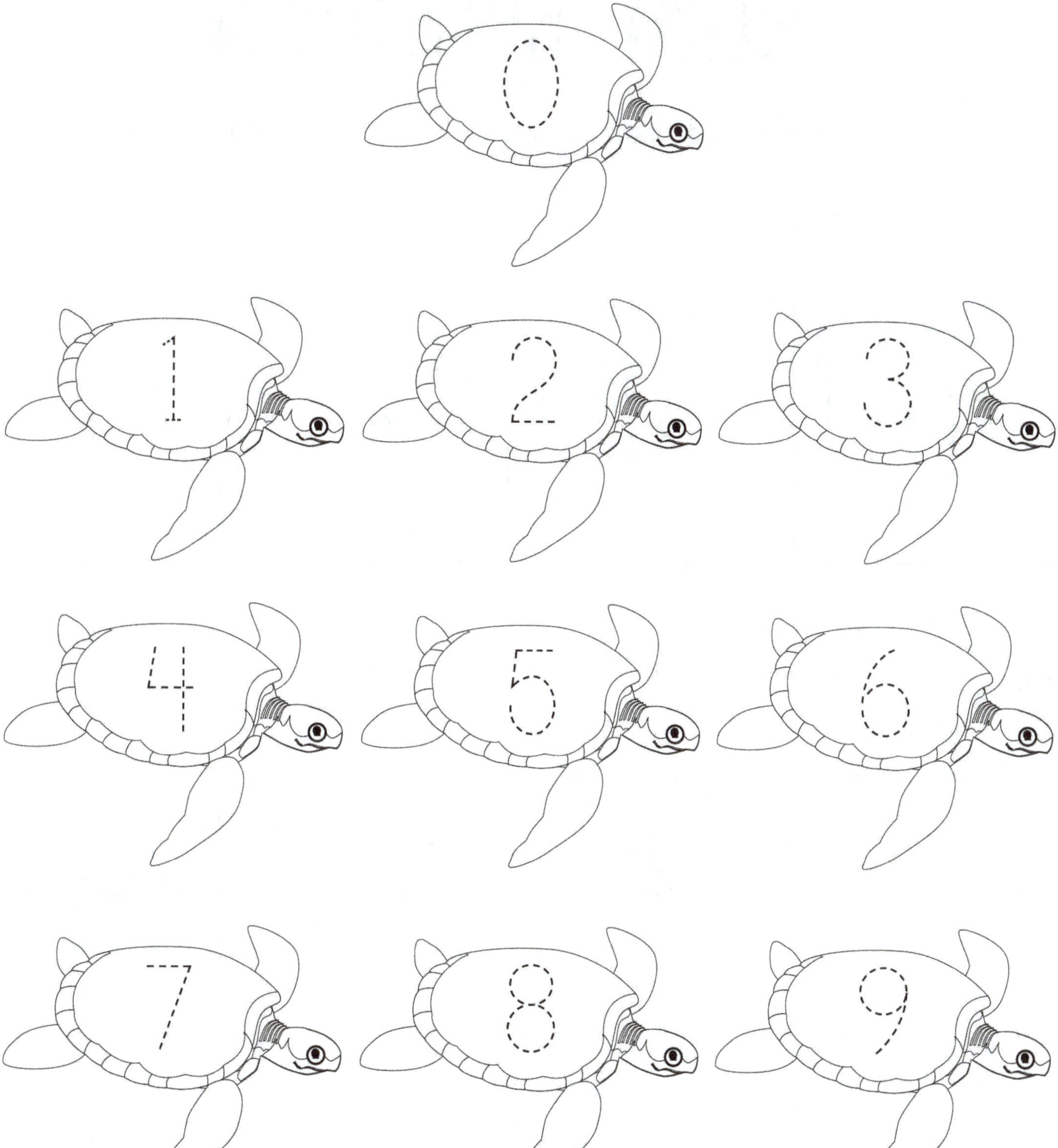

LIFE CYCLE OF A SEA TURTLE

Cut out the images at the bottom and paste into the boxes at the top in the correct order

| 1 | 2 | 3 | 4 |

✂ -

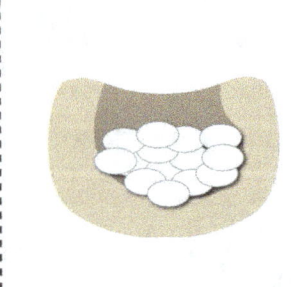   

www.adventuresofscubajack.com

Count

Count the sea turtles then circle the correct answer

2 4 3	5 3 4
6 3 4	3 2 1

www.adventuresofscubajack.com

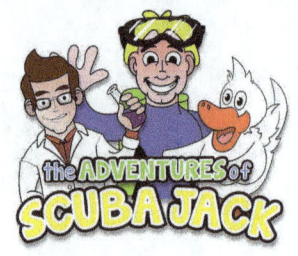

Coloring Activity

www.adventuresofscubajack.com

SEA TURTLE DOT TO DOT

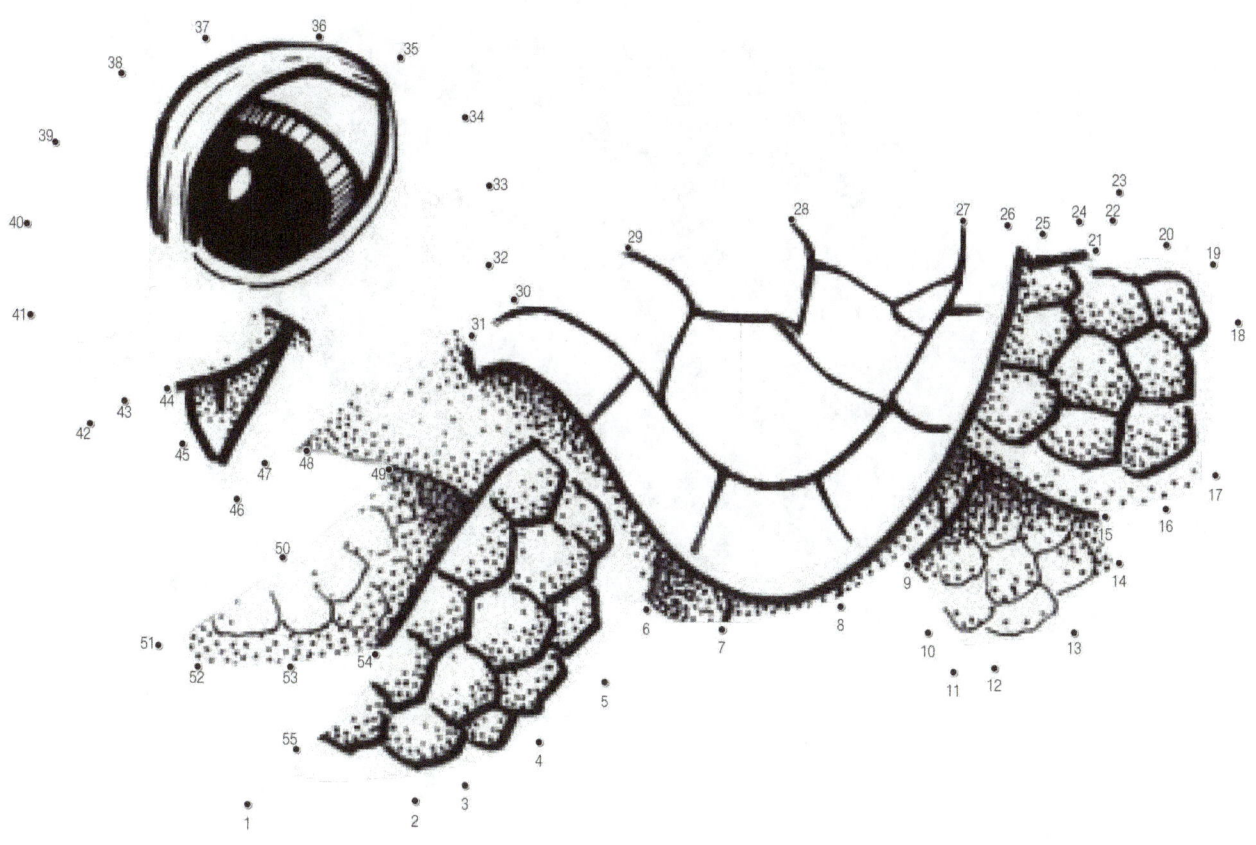

www.adventuresofscubajack.com

SEA TURTLE
LACING CARD

www.adventuresofscubajack.com

COLOR THE TURTLE

www.adventuresofscubajack.com

Visit us at:

www.adventuresofscubajack.com

www.ingramcontent.com/pod-product-compliance
Lightning Source LLC
Chambersburg PA
CBHW060429010526
44118CB00017B/2416